Thoughts of the Oppressive Mind

Dianna Collier

BookLeaf Publishing

India | USA | UK

Presentation by *BookLeaf Publishing*

Web: www.bookleafpub.com

E-mail: info@bookleafpub.com

ISBN: 9789363318397

First edition 2024

*This book is dedicated to God for he gives me
the strength and knowledge to help those in
need and to spread his word.*

ACKNOWLEDGEMENT

Thanks to my husband Rick who listens to my poems and inspires me to continue my writing.

PREFACE

Expressions of thoughts and feelings weighing heavily on the mind or spirit, causing depression or discomfort, profound loneliness or oppressive emptiness.

Addiction

Am I an addictive personality
Is It Hereditary
Do I follow the same path
Even with the generation gap

Hiding from those I love
Want to fly like a dove
Pretending all is alright
Hidden out of sight

Alcohol eases my pain
Helps to calm my brain
Feel like I am on a string
Hiding from everything

Mary Jane nothings greater
Grown in nature
Friends gather in a circle
Smoking and being verbal

The white line has joined the family
Calamity and Insanity
Energy when I am drained
Keeping me on its chain

Joined the wagon train
Out in the rain
Eventually to return
As I will start to yearn

Blasted

Blasted again
Finding my Zen
Don't think anyone will cry
Won't stop until I die

Cocaine is my white line
Finishing a bottle with a sigh
Coughing from my joint
Wondering what's the point

Hiding the truth
Pain and Abuse
Always wanting the day to end
So I can go to bed

Why do I have to feel grief
Why do I need this release
Running out the door
I can't take no more

When life is rough
Just give me my stuff
Money will be found
When the dealer is around

Hiding my addictions
Living with contradictions
Using can cause friction
Living with my restrictions

Can't function within my day
Won't put it away
Don't know what to say
Just doing it my way

The Rush

5

The things we will do
To feel the rush of life
The adrenaline pumping
The tightening in the gut

The Risk
The Reward
Is It Worth It
I think it is

Will we be caught
Will we be arrested
The Fear
The Anxiety

We travel on
Hoping and Praying
With God to Protect
Get us home safely

If success
Happiness and Joy
If not ruin
Police and Jail time

Fear of Nightmares

One reason for my addiction
My constant affliction
Nightmares since youth
Truths and Abuse

My dreams
Make me scream
Horrifying scenes
Going to extremes

When I don't sleep deep
I will wake up and weep
Sometimes I am naked
Frightened then awakened

Enemies can be vicious
Situations malicious
Nothing but misfortune
Leading me to exhaustion

The dreams are in familiar places
With car and foot chases
Terrifying aliens in the sky
Falling from great height trying to fly

Another night of the unknown
Turning my heart to stone
Dreams where you die
Wake up and cry

God please take care of me
To forget all that I see
Don't let it be a part of me
Give me peace and set me free

Hot Flashes

Everyday I feel the heat
Body is so hot I can't sleep
Need to be cold
Feel like I want to explode

Overheating I can't control
Getting cool is my goal
Need the cooling to begin
Heat is trapped in my head

Sweat builds on my face
Spreading everyplace
Stress and anxiety causing heat
Clothes feel tight, sweating in defeat

Striping off my clothes
Throw them on the floor
Coolness of the sheets
To the body is a treat

Stickiness and heavy air
Chokes me without a care
Air conditioner brings relief
I think I can finally sleep

Married at 60

Will the pain ever leave
Will I always grieve
Trust will need returned
Wonder what I have learned

Thoughts of them together
Haunts me every day forever
Take a pill
Kill the pain and deal

Heart will always be broken
Can't be healed by words spoken
Thoughts of being with someone else
Fear and anxiety are felt

When I think of myself
Mania and depression needing help
When a man looks at me
I wonder what he sees

My waist is wide
My hair no longer shines
Lost the bright light in my eyes
When noticed I am surprised

My smile is rare
You can tell I don't care
Even though I try my best
I don't measure up to the rest

The mirror is cold
As I grow old
Time has caught up to me
Have to accept what I see

The Mirror

Don't look like before
Don't recognize my face no more
White smile has dimmed
No longer slim

Eyes are showing signs
Multiple fine lines
Mouth, eyes, all around
Want to scream but no sound

My hair is dull
My pores clogged
My lips are thin
My nose too big

I am still in there
Am I losing my hair
Surgery will not be
As it won't change me

Wear nice clothes to distract
I can't deny the facts
Want to age gracefully
Changing into the older me

Over the Hill

I see I gained it back
Calorie restriction lack
A big ass I see
When I look at me

Two big humps
Not even a bubble butt
My arms wiggle
My thighs jiggle

My boobs droop
Watch them swoop
Scars and Sores
Beautiful skin no more

My fingers are riddled
My nails are brittle
My hands are wrinkled
If I cough I tinkle

AARP is my group
Keeps me in the loop
Meds and illness is our talk
To tired to take a walk

Donuts and Pastries for me
Want to eat all I see
Stress and Anxiety
Caused by Society

Besides having no self-control
Hurting my soul
The scale is my enemy
As it mocks me

Weight loss no luck
No more bucks
Feeling stuck
Old age sucks

Insane Choice

In an insane world
It was the sanest choice
Why lose it all over pride
Take it all in stride

Happiness is a choice
Forgiveness can be given
Trust can be earned
Respect can be gained

Change can happen
Religion can be found
It has to be desired
Working until you expire

Respect gave, needs returned
Truth must be told
Secrets can't be kept
Relationships must be built

Others Forgotten
Friends to Acquaintances
Sharing Responsibility
Building Day by Day

A Kept Woman

Need space
Air to breathe
Wash, Clothe
Feed Me

What, Where, Why
I am asked
He only wants the facts
Always watching my back

Kept is what it is called
Held by years of love
Passion, desire and misery
Promises to the Lord above

Brooding and crying
What about me
For me it cannot be
He must always be

Anger is his weapon
Fear his control
Crying to stop a fight
Silence to shame

Pouts when I leave
Guilt when you go out
Always in his sight
Constantly by his side

Who you going out with
When you coming home
What am I going to do
Where am I going to eat

A puppet on a string
Being guided through the day
Doing what others say
With gentle movements I obey

Your happiness goes first
Then anger
Then silence
Control has been accepted

Don't worry
I will do what I am supposed to do
I will say what I am supposed to say
I will be what I am supposed to be

I hate myself
For submitting to his will
I have no strength left
To fight for my rights

I need out of here
Run until I am clear
Sorry Dear
I need a beer

Rollercoaster of Life

Life is a rollercoaster
Large-small ups-downs
Seen-unseen twists-turns
Unexpected Loop de Loops

Right when you think you know what is next
A big drop happens which shakes you all around
You hold on for dear life
Screaming with weeping along the way

Then hallelujah it all heads up hill
Sometimes it changes slowly
Another with the speed of light
You raise your hands in the air

You cry with joy and glee
Enjoying the ride
Fearful of the next drop
Hoping the ride won't stop

Speaking of Depression

Speaking of depression
Sharing thoughts of suicide
Subject is changed, uncomfortable silence
No help received

Cutting your wrist in the tub
Hanging from the rafters
Bullet in the mouth
Driving into a wall

It is the medicine you see
That has this effect on me
I can't blame it alone
As my life is a cyclone

Therapy can be helpful
Talking of the past
Learning what you truly feel
Being honest with yourself

Alcohol and drugs
Bad choices and DUI's
Poor relationships
Financial distress

They say time heals
Life goes on
Learn to live with your choices
Only worry about what you can control

Does the advice help
Do we ever heal
Can we truly forgive
Only time will tell

Amen

The Waves

Help me I'm drowning
Waves are closing in
Cannot swim anymore
Arms are tired, legs are weak

Try to keep swimming
Going nowhere
Tide needs to change
Travel up-stream

Every time I catch a breath
A new wave comes crashing down
Hearing the roar in my head
Feeling my body shake

Continuing to inhale water
Wishing for fresh air
The sky is darkening
My breath is gone

Manic Mind

Mind is rushing
Thinking about something
Thoughts are always wondering
Head is buzzing

Laying in bed
Twisting and Turning
Blanket to the left
To the right, then left

Too hot, Too cold
Pain intense
Just can't sleep
Finally getting out of bed

Day after Day
I can't sleep again
Insomnia the cause
Brain a fog

Zooming around the house
Room to Room
Trying to do everything at once
Not getting it all done

Go until I fall
Go until I am sick
Go until I make mistakes
It's all I can take

Finally falling into bed
Pain in my head
Pray for sleep
It is in my reach

Trapped

Trapped let me out
What is this about
I can't open the door
Can't be in the sun no more

Open windows for fresh air
Too tired to brush my hair
Feels life is unfair
Just want to stay in my liar

Want to go out and play
Maybe not today
My property is my border
Outside brings fear and disorder

Standing at the sidelines
As life goes by
Chores are done
Too tired for fun

Anxiety makes decisions switch
Reasons I can ditch
Wedding and parties missed
Gifts and cards dismissed

Friends miss me
Family unseen
I miss them
Life unlived

Fatigue

As I struggle to write this text
Exhausted not wanting to do what's next
Trying so hard to do my best
Needing to get some rest

Never a day off
Can't have it soft
Everyday is hard
Being dealt this card

Working all day
With constant delays
Chores have to be done
Can't get out in the sun

Caring for others
Feel like being smothered
Watching as other suffer
New things being uncovered

Losing yourself every day
Not having a say
Doing things another's way
Not even getting paid

Someday I will miss these days
As the one's I love are away
Leaving me all alone
Crying and missing my own

Forgetful

Moving through the house
My mind doubts
Walking through the day
My thoughts are astray

Forgetting things as I go
Pots left on the stove
Dogs forgot in their crate
Work undone they have to wait

Did I take my pills
Forgot to pay my bills
Who am I supposed to call
Feel like I am crawling up a wall

What time is it
I think I need to sit
Chest pains and arm hurts
I think I might burst

My day is through
Sleep is due
Thoughts in my head
Another night awake I'll spend

Giving until you break

Bow, Wow, Wow
Now, Now, Now
The horse pulls the plow
Using every part of the cow

They drain me to a husk
Leaving my mind as mush
Cannot get through the day
No one listens to what I say

My biggest concern is when I die
I know they will have to try
Get their ass out of bed
Their own burden they have to tread

Their needs always come first
Sometimes I feel cursed
All I do is move my toe
The dogs have to go

I finally fall into bed
Laying down my head
My mind will not rest
Falling asleep doing my best

Low in the Day

My mind is a fog
Can't even sing a song
My eyes are dim
Closing my eye lids

My strength dwindles
Need some minerals
My body feels weak
Just want to sleep

Too tired to play
Can't go out today
Responsibilities in the way
Work and get paid

My spirit is broken
Hoping it will be awaken
But it is not so
Thoughts I cannot let go

Of me much is asked
So, I can't relax
My mind tells me to fly
Even though I know it is not time

Up Again

Up again all night long
Singing myself songs
Tired of laying in bed
Thoughts going through my head

So I will get up
Even though it is rough
Working on piles of stuff
Knowing the morning will be tough

Naps during the day
If he would stay
Only a brief relief
I would get some sleep

So sad but don't know why
Anything I will try
Going to bed all baked
Don't want to be awake

My nights are days
My days are night
We try to have it all
Worry our downfall

Darkness in sight
Black, grey, white
Here comes the blues
There's nothing I can do

I give up
All broke up
Fall to the floor
Not doing this no more

Restless

Take a cruise through the river bends
Drive across the countryside
Lay on the beach
Sleep under the stars

See the Cathedrals of Rome
The site of the Crucifixion
The birth of Christ
A dip in the Dead Sea

The green of Ireland
The Castles of England
The Mystery of Asia
The Wilds of Africa

Run through a field of daisies
Live by the waterside
A log cabin full of happiness
The mountains is our view

A time will come when I can live
A time will come when I can dream
A time will come when I can be seen
I feel the restlessness in me